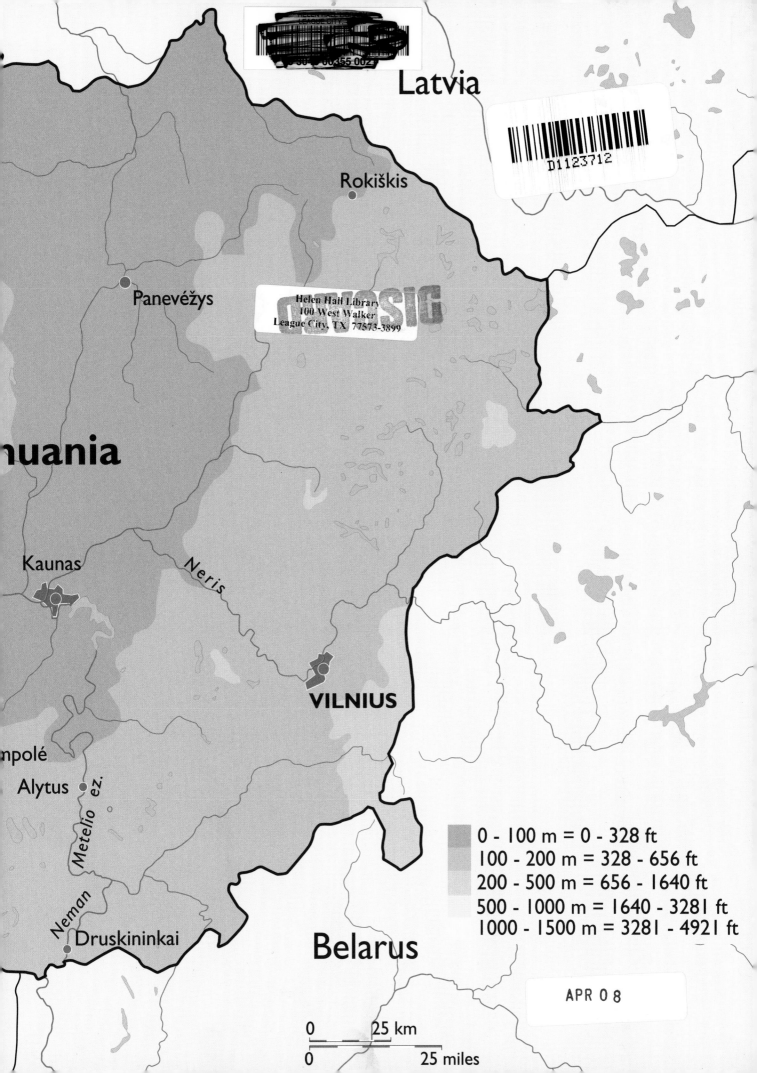

Latvia

Rokiškis

Panevėžys

thuania

Kaunas

Neris

VILNIUS

mpolé

Alytus   Metelio ez.

Metelio

Neman

Druskininkai

Belarus

0 - 100 m = 0 - 328 ft
100 - 200 m = 328 - 656 ft
200 - 500 m = 656 - 1640 ft
500 - 1000 m = 1640 - 3281 ft
1000 - 1500 m = 3281 - 4921 ft

APR 0 8

0   25 km

0   25 miles

Looking at Europe

Lithuania

Jan Willem Bultje

The Oliver Press, Inc.
Minneapolis

This edition published in 2006 by The Oliver Press, Inc.
Charlotte Square
5707 West 36th Street
Minneapolis, MN 55416-2510

Published by arrangement with KIT Publishers, The Netherlands, and
The Evans Publishing Group, London, UK, 2005

Library of Congress Cataloging-in-Publication Data

Bultje, Jan Willem.
    Lithuania / Jan Willem Bultje.
        p. cm. -- (Looking at Europe)
    Includes index.
    Contents: History -- The country -- Towns and cities -- People and culture -- Education
-- Cuisine -- Transportation -- The economy -- Tourism -- Nature.
    ISBN 1-881508-43-9
    1. Lithuania--Juvenile literature. I. Title. II. Series.

DK505.23.B85 2006
947.93--dc22

                                                                                    2006040093

Text: Jan Willem Bultje
Photographs: Jan Willem Bultje
Translation: Wilma Hoving
US editing: Holly Day
Design and Layout: Grafisch Ontwerpbureau Agaatsz BNO, Meppel, The Netherlands
Cover: Icon Productions, Minneapolis, USA
Cartography: Armand Haye, Amsterdam, The Netherlands
Production: J & P Far East Productions, Soest, The Netherlands

Picture Credits
All images courtesy of KIT Publishers except:
p. 18 (b) Aigars Jansons, p. 30 (b) Normunds Mezins, p. 34 (t) en 44 (b) Gatis Diezins: EPAa
Photo, AFI; p. 9(b) © Hulton-Deutsch Collection/CORBIS

ISBN 1-881508-43-9
Printed in Singapore
10 09 08 07 06   8 7 6 5 4 3 2 1

Contents

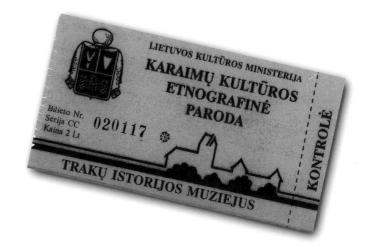

Introduction

Lithuania – officially the Republic of Lithuania – is one of the Baltic states, located in north central Europe. Lithuania is bordered by Latvia in the north, Belarus in the east, Poland in the south, and Kaliningrad – an area that belongs to Russia – in the southwest. Its western border is the Baltic Sea. The capital and largest city is Vilnius.

Although the land was settled as early as the Stone Age, the various Lithuanian tribes were not unified until the thirteenth century. From that time, Lithuania grew to become one of the most important states in medieval Europe, largely because of the trade in amber, which can still be found in many places across the region, and on which other countries placed a high value. By 1569, however, its power had declined and it was merged with Poland. Later, Poland itself was partitioned, and present-day Lithuania was absorbed into the Russian Empire. Like the other Baltic states – Estonia and Latvia – Lithuania enjoyed a brief period as an independent republic between the two World Wars, but was reabsorbed into the Soviet Union, or USSR, in 1944, when it was known as the Lithuanian Soviet Socialist Republic. In the following years, Lithuania was subject to a Soviet communist regime, and it was only in 1991 that the country was granted independence once again.

▶ *Lithuania is a land of water. There are more than 3,000 lakes in the country, most of them in the eastern regions. This is the lake at Zarasaičio.*

The influence of the various peoples who have conquered and settled in Lithuania is still evident. Russian and Polish are widely used languages, and under the Polish influence, Roman Catholicism is still the dominant religion. However, since the nineteenth century, there has been a revival of interest in Lithuanian culture and traditions, and today the people celebrate their heritage in many ways, including festivals, literature, and other forms of the arts.

In December of 2002, Lithuania became a member of NATO. The principles of security and international co-operation between the organization's member states has allowed the Lithuanian government to stop focusing on external affairs that might affect their country and instead to concentrate on rebuilding and establishing infrastructures that will directly benefit its own people. Such initiatives include improvements in transportation systems, reviewing and improving the education and legal systems, and restoring many old buildings that suffered damage during the long periods of occupation.

In a 2004 referendum, 91 percent of the Lithuanian people voted in favor of the country joining the European Union (EU), and in May of that year it was accepted as a full member of the organization. The entry of Lithuania into the EU has been significant. It has opened up a number of opportunities for developing international relations. Previously, Russia had been Lithuania's main trading partner, and the country suffered during the period of Soviet unrest in the late 1990s; today, its economy is recovering thanks to new trade relations with other European countries and beyond.

◀ *Klaipeda is an old coastal resort. It is one of the most popular tourist destinations because of its historic buildings and its location on the Baltic coast.*

History

The first people ventured into the territory that is now Lithuania after the end of the last Ice Age, and from the Stone Age – around 9000 BC – hunters from southern and western parts of Europe roamed the area.

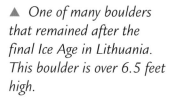

As time passed, the land dried out and became more habitable. Other peoples moved into the area, particularly from central Russia. Around 2000 BC, a tribe of farmers described as the *Bandkeramik* entered the region from the Middle East. The name is German, and stems from the characteristic designs of linear bands on the pottery made by these people. We do not know what they called themselves, but they were the first group to establish farming communities in Lithuania. They grew peas, flax, and wheat. They also raised livestock – pigs, goats, sheep, and cows. The transition from hunters and gatherers to farmers was a gradual one, but these hunters learned about farming from the new tribes.

▲ *One of many boulders that remained after the final Ice Age in Lithuania. This boulder is over 6.5 feet high.*

Gold of the North

By around 500 BC, a lively trade had grown up around the discovery of amber, which was found all over the region – in Poland and the Baltic countries. Amber is the fossilized remains of ancient tree-resin. It is very lightweight and over 40 million years old. It was nicknamed the "Gold of the North," and was used to make jewelry. The Roman Empire had a high demand for amber, and it was also transported to Greece and Egypt. The golden age of the amber trade lasted from AD 100 until AD 500.

Around this time, the Baltic region began to suffer invasion from various peoples. The Slavs were repelled, but the Vikings began a series of attacks around AD 600. They were attracted by the amber, and began to trade with people living in the areas that are now Russia and the Ukraine. Their trade route ran along the Daugava River in Lithuania, and became very important in the eighth and ninth centuries.

◄ *Amber has been turned into items of jewelry since Roman times and is still used today. All over Lithuania, shops sell pieces crafted from amber.*

▶ *The Crusader Knights, who tried to oust the Muslims from the Holy Land*

The Teutonic Order

The next people to attempt to conquer the area were the Russians. Although they did not succeed, the 200 years spent trying to settle in Lithuania, Latvia, and Estonia saw the establishment of the Orthodox religion in the area. At that time, the Baltic peoples were made up of two major tribes – the Žemaitija in the west and the Aukštaitija in the east and southeast. A number of cities in this region, such as Riga and Tallinn, joined the Hanseatic League, a politically powerful union of German, Dutch, English, and Scandinavian trading towns.

At around the same time, two German military orders – the Livonian Brothers of the Sword and the Teutonic Knights – moved into the region, and eventually they joined together. Initially set up as a brotherhood of knights and priests, the Teutonic Order took care of the wounded and sick during the Christian Crusades to the Holy Land. However, by the end of the twelfth century, it had been converted into a genuine order of knights, with a clear-cut goal – the conversion of Prussian and Baltic pagans and the conquest of their territories. In the middle of the thirteenth century, the leader of the Aukštaitija, Duke Mindaugas, united all the Lithuanian tribes so they could defend themselves against the German knights. To prevent the knights from gaining too much influence, he had himself baptised and "converted" to Christianity, but this was just for show – in reality, he and his people remained pagans.

During this period, the Teutonic Knights suffered a series of defeats against the Russians and Lithuanians, and they slowly retreated. By 1309, they had withdrawn and set up their headquarters at Malbork in Poland, although skirmishes between the Baltic and Polish peoples and the knights continued for several years. Under Mindaugas' successor, Gediminas, Lithuania became an important European power with a multinational and multicultural society. Parts of Russia and present-day Latvia were absorbed into the Grand Duchy of Lithuania.

Through the marriages of Lithuanian princes with Polish princesses, the two countries formed a close relationship, and in 1385 they created an official union. Jogaila of Lithuania was appointed head of this new commonwealth on the condition that he converted his people to Christianity. Lithuania was the last European country to renounce paganism and adopt the Christian faith.

◀ *On this old map, Lithuanian territories stretch as far as the Black Sea.*

The Polish-Lithuanian Commonwealth

After Jogaila's death, the Lithuanian rulers increasingly lost their power to Poland. In 1569, Poland and Lithuania became one state, the Polish-Lithuanian Commonwealth. Krakow, in Poland, was made its capital. From this time onwards, the upper classes began to speak Polish, and Polish culture was adopted by many people of Lithuanian descent. Lithuanian peasants suffered the most, as they became serfs working on land belonging to the wealthy Polish nobility.

In the neighboring Baltic states, Estonia and Latvia, the Swedes gained control. Russia, aiming to expand its territories westward, fought against the Swedes for control of the Baltic countries. During the Great Northern War (1700–21), Sweden lost Estonia and Latvia to Russia.

In 1795, Polish-Lithuanian independence ended. Prussia captured the western part of Lithuania, and the remaining lands came under the rule of the Russian tsar. The French emperor Napoleon also paid a visit to the region – in 1812, while retreating from an unsuccessful attack on Moscow, he took leave of his army in Vilnius to return to France. Throughout the nineteenth century, the Polish army made several attempts to free Lithuania from Russian rule, notably in 1830 and 1863. However, they were defeated by the Russians.

▲ A view of old Kaunas seen from the hill on the opposite bank of the River Neman. Kaunas was a medieval trading post, and was acquired by Russia during the third Partition of Poland in 1795.

The Russians left their mark on Lithuanian society. They wanted to banish all Polish influences. The Roman Catholic Church was suppressed, the Latin alphabet was banned, and only books printed in the Cyrillic alphabet (using Russian script) were allowed. In the seaport of Memel (present-day Klaipeda), which was Prussian at that time, Lithuanian books were smuggled into the country, allowing the people to at least retain a small part of their own history and culture. The Lithuanian people staged frequent uprisings against their Russian overlords.

National consciousness

Despite foreign rule, the three Baltic countries began to regain their national consciousness in the second half of the nineteenth century. Poetry was written in their own languages, and an interest in national history arose. By the time the First World War broke out in 1914, Lithuania, Latvia, and Estonia had all determined to fight for the right to be independent states.

During the First World War, Lithuania was occupied by the Germans, but Lithuanians still sought ways to gain autonomous rule. Toward the end of the war, it became clear that the German and Russian empires were collapsing, and on February 16, 1918, Lithuania was proclaimed an independent republic. Germany however, was reluctant to give up its influence, and put forward a German prince to be crowned as the new king of Lithuania. Wilhelm von Urach, Count of Würtemberg, became King Mindaugas II. His reign was brief. On November 11, 1918, Germany surrendered, the war came to an end, and so did German influence in Lithuania.

Poland tried to regain power in Lithuania, but the Lithuanian army defeated them in most parts of the country. However, the Poles occupied the capital, Vilnius, and its surrounding area between 1920 until 1939. During that period, Kaunas was Lithuania's capital.

▲ *Signing the treaty between Germany and the Soviet Union, known as the Molotov-Ribbentrop Pact, in which Lithuania was granted to the Soviet Union.*

The Second World War

During the Second World War (1939–45), Lithuanian territory was fought over by Germany and the Soviet Union. On August 23, 1939, the two countries signed a non-aggression pact – the leaders agreed that Germany would claim Poland and the Soviet Union would gain possession of the Baltic countries. On September 1, 1939, German troops marched into Poland, and the Red Army (the Soviets) entered Lithuania on September 17. Thousands of people were taken prisoner and deported to the Soviet Union. A communist government was installed.

However, Germany attacked the Soviet Union on June 22, 1941, and Lithuania came under German rule again. Over 100,000 Jews were captured, many of them from Vilnius, which had been known as the "Jerusalem of the East" before the war because of its high Jewish population. In July of 1944, Lithuania again fell under Soviet rule and became one of the Soviet republics.

◀ *German troops march through the streets of Memel (Klaipeda) in 1939.*

▲ *Gediminas Prospekt in the capital city of Vilnius*

Independence

For the next 40 years, Lithuania existed under Soviet communist rule. However, toward the end of the 1980s, under President Mikhail Gorbachev, a process known as *glasnost* (which means "openness") began in the Soviet Union. This led to more freedom, and under its influence various groups in Lithuania got together to fight for their country's independence. By 1989, the barriers between the communist countries in the East and the democratic West were breaking down. The following year, the independent state of Lithuania was declared, but the Soviet Union – still officially in power – launched an attack, and several people were killed. Soviet rule was on its last legs, though, and in September 1991, it officially recognized Lithuanian independence. On September 17, Lithuania became a member of the United Nations, securing its status as a free republic.

▼ *A monument to the people who died in the Soviet attacks in reaction to Lithuania's declaration of independence in 1990*

The country

With an area of 25,200 square miles, Lithuania is the largest and most southerly of the three Baltic states. From north to south it measures about 162 miles, and from east to west about 225. In the official language of the country, it is called Lietuvos Respublika.

Lithuania's landscape is mostly flat, made up of fertile lowlands which are good for agriculture. There are two ranges of hills, one in the north and one in the south, but nothing that comes close to being mountainous. The average height of these hills is 500 feet. The highest point in the country, at 958 feet, is Juozapines Hill, to the east of the capital, Vilnius, near the border with Belarus. Nearly a quarter of the country is covered with forests and woodland.

Lithuania's coastline on the Baltic Sea, in the west, is about 62 miles long. More than half the coastline is sheltered by a sandbar, 2 miles wide, called the Curonian Spit. The water between the mainland and the sandbar is known as the Curonian Lagoon.

▼ Most of Lithuania's landscape is flat lowland plains. Farms can be found across these wide-open spaces as the soil is very fertile and good for growing crops.

◀ Sand dunes line the beaches, offering protection from the winds, which can be icy cold in winter. In some places the dunes are as high as 197 feet.

◀ *The River Neman (Nemunas in Lithuanian) begins its course in Belarus and flows westward through Lithuania. Here, it runs past the spa resort Birštonas.*

Rivers and lakes

There are many rivers in Lithuania. The Neman River – known as the Nemunas in Lithuanian and the Memel in German – is the longest in the country, at 582 miles. The river rises in Belarus near Minsk, flows past the city of Kaunas in Lithuania, and enters the Baltic Sea on the borders of Lithuania and Kaliningrad. Other major rivers in Lithuania include the Neris and the Venta. However, despite all these waterways, only 375 miles of Lithuania's rivers are navigable by boat.

Lithuania has nearly 3,000 lakes, most of which are found in the eastern part of the country. The largest lake is Druksiai (17.5 square miles) and the deepest is Tauragnas (198 feet).

▼ *Some of Lithuania's lakes are several miles in length. In the summer, it is possible to swim in many of them, although the water can be cold.*

Climate

Lithuania's climate is relatively mild, but it differs between coastal and inland areas. The coastal regions have a maritime climate, which means that there is not an extreme difference in temperatures between winter and summer, and humidity is relatively high.

Inland regions have a continental climate, where there are distinct seasons, and temperatures vary more between winter and summer. Countries with a continental climate have relatively little rainfall.

In the summer – from May to August – temperatures inland can reach 86°F, but on the coast it is usually cooler than this.

▲ *Spring begins in April, with small flowers carpeting the woodland floors.*

Winters are long, lasting from November to March. There is often a harsh frost, and throughout the winter months snow lies thick on the ground. Lithuania's many lakes and ponds often freeze over. Freezing rain and snowstorms can occur. It is particularly cold in the east, where winter temperatures can drop to -13°F. Coastal temperatures in the winter are higher, however, as the influence of the Gulf Stream brings warmer air to the Baltic coast.

Spring is short, and after the snow has melted in April, flowers and plants seem to pop up out of the ground almost overnight. Autumn begins in September, which is usually rainy with low temperatures. Annual rainfall averages 29 inches along the coast and 20 inches inland.

▶ *The Nemunas is the largest river in Lithuania. It rises in Belarus and flows trough Lithuania to the Baltic Sea.*

Towns and cities

Lithuania is divided into 10 counties, each named after its principal city. Although the country has a lot of farmland and wide-open spaces, there are still 92 cities altogether in Lithuania, five of which have more than 100,000 inhabitants.

Vilnius

Vilnius is Lithuania's capital, and its largest city, with around 550,000 inhabitants. It is located in a hilly landscape at the confluence of the Neris and Vilnia rivers. The city was officially founded in 1323, when the Grand Duke Gediminas chose it as his center and built a castle there. Many of the streets are narrow and winding, particularly in the older parts of the city.

▲ *A narrow lane runs through the old town in Vilnius.*

▼ *St. Stanislaus Cathedral stands on the site of an old Gothic church, built on the orders of Duke Jogaila after he had converted to Christianity. The church was destroyed by fire, but has since been rebuilt and restored to its present form. The belfry stands apart from the church.*

Over the centuries, Vilnius has been devastated by fire, plague, and war. It fell under Russian rule in 1795, and grew to be an important center of Jewish learning in the nineteenth century. After the Second World War, it became part of the Soviet Union, and many of the old buildings were neglected and fell into decay. Today, some of these are being restored.

The old town is the true historical center of Vilnius, and has buildings in several architectural styles. Vilnius University, established by the Jesuits in 1579, is located in the center of the old town. It is one of the oldest universities in Eastern Europe. Among other sights in Vilnius, are the churches – more than 40 of them, including St. Stanislaus Cathedral – most built in the Baroque style.

Among the most popular sites in Vilnius is Gediminas Castle, which the Lithuanians have adopted as one of their symbols. It appears on the national currency (lita).

▲ Gediminas Tower stands on the 157-foot-high Castle Hill. From here, all the passing ships could be seen.

◀ Gediminas Prospekt is one of the busiest streets in Vilnius. It has been opened for pedestrians, and is lined with shops, restaurants, banks, and government buildings.

Kaunas

Kaunas is the second-largest Lithuanian city, located approximately 50 miles from Vilnius, and with 380,000 inhabitants. Like the capital, Kaunas has been built at the confluence of two rivers, the Neris and the Neman.

Kaunas was founded in the eleventh century, and grew to be an important trading post in medieval times. It was also a Lithuanian stronghold during the people's resistance to the Teutonic Knights (see page 7). Since that time, Kaunas has been subjected to various foreign oppressors, including the Poles, the Swedes, the Russians, and the French. Napoleon's army plundered the city on retreat from Russia in 1812. Kaunas has therefore been rebuilt several times in its history.

▼ *Around the outside of Town Hall Square are several old merchant houses. The house on the left is the old pharmacy.*

▲ *In the middle of Town Hall Square stands the town hall itself, which has been nicknamed the "white swan."*

An example of Renaissance architecture in Kaunas

Between 1920 and 1939, Kaunas was the capital of Lithuania, as Vilnius was under Polish occupation. Like many of Lithuania's cities, it suffered under Soviet rule. During this time, many churches and educational establishments were closed or used for other purposes. It was only in 1990 that the Vytautas Magnus University in the city re-opened and the churches began to offer mass again. Among the best-known churches in the city are the Jesuit church on the south side of Town Hall Square, and the large cathedral a short distance away.

In the Middle Ages, stone houses were banned in Klaipeda, and only wooden ones could be built. When the city was under attack and threatened to fall, the inhabitants could set it on fire, leaving nothing for the enemy. That is why there are no Gothic or Renaissance buildings to be found in Klaipeda. It was only in more recent times that stone buildings were permitted.

Klaipeda

The seaport, Klaipeda (also known by its German name, Memel) is Lithuania's third-largest city, and is located on the Baltic coast at the end of the Curonian Spit (see page 11). Around 194,000 people live in Klaipeda. In the thirteenth century, the city was controlled by the Teutonic Knights. Later, it became Prussian territory until the end of the First World War and was occupied by German forces during the Second World War. The German influence is still noticeable in Klaipeda.

Klaipeda is one of the oldest cities in Lithuania, and there has been a settlement here since the seventh century. Today, it is a key industrial center, as well as a port, with shipyards and industries manufacturing textiles, fertilizers, and timber products.

◄ *The port of Klaipeda, in western Lithuania, is the base for a large fishing fleet.*

◀ About six miles from Siauliai lies the Hill of Crosses. Thousands of crosses have been erected here since medieval times, and it has long been a place of pilgrimage for the Lithuanian people.

Siauliai

Siauliai lies in northern Lithuania, and is the country's fourth-largest city, with around 134,000 inhabitants. Large parts of it were destroyed by Napoleon's army in 1812, and during the Second World War, 80 percent of the city was ruined. There is little left now of the old town, although some of the old streets are still there. The Renaissance tower of the Cathedral of St. Peter and St. Paul, standing 230 feet high, dominates the city skyline.

Although much of the architecture dates from the post-war period and lacks the beauty of that in other parts of the country, this is still the cultural center of northern Lithuania. Various festivals and exhibitions are held in Siauliai throughout the year. The city is a rail hub and another of Lithuania's industrial centers, with shoe manufacturers and flax-processing factories. It is also home to the Gubernija brewery, which was established in 1786.

Panevézys

Panevézys, located in the middle of Lithuania, has around 120,000 inhabitants. The city suffered particularly during the First World War, and there are few historical buildings left. Instead, there are several large businesses, producing textiles, furniture, food, glass, and motor parts.

▶ Siauliai is the most important cultural and industrial center in northern Lithuania.

People and culture

Lithuania has a population of nearly 3.6 million, and 80 percent of the people are of Lithuanian origin. Around 70 percent of the population lives in the larger cities. The population density is around 144 people per square mile.

▼ *Although the majority of the population is concentrated in the cities, many older people live in the countryside, in villages or farmhouses.*

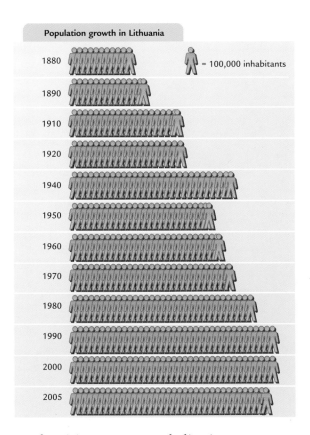

Population growth in Lithuania

1880
1890
1910
1920
1940
1950
1960
1970
1980
1990
2000
2005

= 100,000 inhabitants

In the cities, most people live in apartments rather than houses. However, it is common for Lithuanian people to own cottages in the countryside, which they visit in summer. These country cottages often stay in families for generations, and townspeople enjoy spending time there, tending the gardens or the orchards, which they are unable to do in the cities.

Ethnic groups

The largest minority group is Russian (almost 9 percent), followed by the Poles (7 percent), and Belarusians (1.6 percent); 2.4 percent belong to other groups. In all, there are more than 100 different nationalities living in Lithuania.

Before the Second World War, there were around 300,000 Jews in Lithuania, but between 1941 and 1944, most of them were transported to concentration or labor camps, where thousands died. Lithuania lost almost one million people through acts of war, deportation, and emigration between 1940 and 1958. More than three million Lithuanians live abroad. Around 800,000 of them have settled in the USA. Other large Lithuanian communities can be found in Canada, South America, the UK, and Australia.

Language

Lithuanian (an Indo-European language of the same family as most of those used in Europe) only became the country's official language in 1918, and even then it was mainly used for official documents rather than being the common language of the people. Over the years, Polish and then Russian have been the most important languages, as these were the people who ruled large parts of Lithuania. These languages are still widely spoken. In 1989, Lithuanian regained its status as the country's official language. A few Lithuanian dialects are also spoken. Lithuania has long been under the influence of Polish culture and language, and the Lithuanians feel more strongly connected to Europe than the other Baltic states do.

Religion

The majority of the population is Roman Catholic (85 percent). Strong ties with Poland over the centuries prevented Protestant influences coming into the country from nearby Estonia. Before the Second World War, 13 percent of the population was Jewish. Today, only a tiny Jewish community remains compared to the numbers there once were. There has only been any real freedom of religion in Lithuania since it gained independence in 1991.

Some Lithuanian words

Good morning	*Laba rytas*
Yes	*Taip*
No	*Ne*
Thank you	*ačiu*
Post office	*Paštas*
How much is it?	*Kiek kainuoja?*
Street	*Gatvé*
Main street	*Prospektas*
Hotel	*Viešbutis*
Soup	*Sriuba*
Coffee	*Kava*
Mineral water	*Mineralvanduo*

▼ *The interior of one of Vilnius's many Baroque-style churches*

▼ *The Orthodox faith was brought to Lithuania by the Russians many centuries ago, and still has many followers. There are 45 Russian Orthodox parishes in the country.*

Today, as well as the Roman Catholics, there are two small Protestant denominations – the Lutherans and the Calvinists. The Lutherans have around 30 parishes in Lithuania, and the Calvinists have 8. Followers of the Eastern Orthodox faith make up around five percent of the population, drawn mainly from those of Russian descent.

▲ *National newspapers and magazines from Lithuania. People also read magazines imported from other European countries.*

Karaites

At the end of the fourteenth century, Grand Duke Vytautas brought a tribe of people from the Crimea in Russia to Trakai, to work as palace guards. The people belonged to a Jewish sect called the Karaites, which means "followers of the Bible." Karaite Jews only believe what is written in the Old Testament (the Hebrew Bible), and they do not accept the later scriptures. About 400 Karaites still live in the wooden houses of Trakai. They speak their own language and have their own culture and customs. They serve exclusively Karaite specialities in their restaurant.

Media

The most important newspapers in Lithuania are *Lietuvos Rytas*, *Respublika* and *Lietuvos Žinios*. The first of these is the most widely read newspaper in the country. *Panele*, *Women*, and *Veidas* are popular magazines. The LRT (Lithuanian Radio and Television) is the national broadcasting company. There are two television channels and four radio channels, as well as many local stations. Radio programs have been transmitted since 1926, and television programs since 1957, although the second television channel was only launched in 2003. Currently, there are three commercial stations, and several more that can be received through cable.

Amanda has been into town with her friends. She had the day off school today because it is Good Friday. "We bought ice cream treats from a shop," she says. Young people who live near the cities often spend days out of school and weekends hanging around in the town centers, shopping, or just meeting friends for lunch or coffee.

▲ *Every four years, a huge stage is erected in Vingis Park to host the national Song Festival.*

Festivals

The first European song festival took place in Zurich, Switzerland, in 1843. Two years later, a similar event was organized in Würzberg, Germany. However, when Adolf Hitler's National Socialist Party gained power in 1933, the festivals were stopped.

In the Baltic countries, which were under strong German influence, song festivals were also organized, first in Estonia, in 1869, and four years later in Latvia. The first Lithuanian song festival did not take place until after the First World War, when Lithuania gained independence for the first time. The festival was held in Kaunas from August 23-25, 1924.

▼ *Lithuanian festivals are great celebrations of the country's culture and customs. Traditional clothing is worn, and old folksongs are played and sung.*

Since then, the event has become a tradition. Every four years, the song festival is held in Vilnius. A large stage is raised in Vingis Park, which accommodates thousands of people. Nearly 30,000 singers, musicians, and dancers take part in the festival – groups, orchestras, and choirs. As well as modern and classical music, traditional songs are also performed.

The festival opens with a folklore day. People from various regions gather in Sereikiškiu Park, dressed in traditional Lithuanian costumes. They practice old trades, display the traditional crafts made in their village or region, and offer customary drinks and dishes. Dancers from different regions perform traditional dances, and sing their old songs.

In Kalnu Park, a large song and dance feast takes place in the evenings. Around 3,000 people attend the festivities.

▶ *Midsummer is also celebrated in Lithuania, around June 21. It is a lively occasion. Girls pick flowers and make crowns to wear on their heads. Many people wear traditional costumes and dance outside.*

The highlight of the festival is "Dancing Day in Vingis Park." On the large stage, 400 choirs group together. These include youth choirs, children's choirs, male-voice choirs, female-voice choirs, and mixed choirs. They perform songs from old and contemporary composers. The concert lasts for about four hours and concludes with grand harmonized singing by the choirs and audience. This usually goes on for a number of hours.

▲ *People gather from the different regions in Lithuania to celebrate their heritage. The festival concludes with a "dancing day," at which many different choirs and musicians perform.*

◀ *Steponas Darius and Stanislovas Girénas are immortalized on the 10-lita banknote.*

Flying Heroes

Steponas (Steven) Darius and Stanislovas (Stanley) Girénas are two of Lithuania's most celebrated figures. Steponas Darius emigrated to America in 1917, joined the United States Army, and served in France during the First World War. In 1920, he returned to Lithuania, where he took flying lessons at the military academy. In 1927, he was promoted to the rank of captain. In the same year, he returned to the USA and took part in civil aviation.

In 1932, Darius and his compatriot Stanislovas Girénas agreed to fly to Lithuania across the Atlantic Ocean. For what was then 3,200 US dollars, they bought a second-hand Bellnka airplane, fitted it with a new engine, and named it *Lituanica*. The airplane managed to fly at just 125 miles per hour. They left New York on July 15, 1933 – without authorization, because the airplane did not have the right instruments. They did not even have parachutes on board! Navigating simply by using a compass, they left in the direction of the UK, and flew over Scotland the next day. On July 17, they reached Germany, about 62 miles north of Berlin. A few hours later the aircraft crashed, killing both pilots. They had flown nearly 4,050 miles in about 37 hours. The cause of the crash was never discovered. The story of their courageous journey made headlines around the world, placing Lithuania on the world map overnight, and the two men became national heroes.

Government

Lithuania is a parliamentary democracy. It is made up of 10 counties, each with an administrative capital. The counties are subdivided into 44 districts. The Lithuanian parliament is called the Seimas. It has 141 members, who are elected for a four-year term. Not all members are elected directly by the population; 70 members are elected in a nationwide vote, and 71 members are elected indirectly in constituencies. Anyone over the age of 18 can vote in the elections. Members of parliament have to be at least 25 years old. The Lithuanian constitution was adopted in October 1992.

The Social Democratic Coalition is the largest party, with 51 seats; the New Union (Social Liberals) holds 25 seats; the Liberal Union holds 24 seats; the Liberal Democrats hold 13 seats; the Homeland Union (Conservatives) holds nine seats; the Farmers' Party and the New Democracy Party hold 8 seats. There are also several smaller parties. The Cabinet consists of 13 ministers under the chairmanship of the prime minister.

▼ *Most government buildings are located on Gediminas Prospekt, one of the main streets in Vilnius.*

Education

Education in Lithuania is compulsory between the ages of 6 and 16. Although pupils can leave school when they have completed primary and basic secondary education, many choose to continue their studies at senior secondary schools, and then at universities.

Primary education (*Pradiné mokykla*) lasts for four years. It is followed by basic secondary education, which takes place at two different institutions: basic school (*Pagrindiné mokykla*) and secondary school (*Viduriné mokykla*). Basic secondary education lasts for six years. If they choose to, pupils can then go on to senior secondary or vocational secondary schools.

Senior secondary education

Senior secondary education takes place at a secondary school (*Viduriné mokykla*) or a gymnasium (*Gimnazija*). Lithuanian gymnasiums specialize in the humanities (classical and/or contemporary languages, and social sciences), practical arts (natural sciences, technology, and economics), and the fine arts (art and music). The gymnasium diploma allows access to university or higher vocational education, such as teacher-training courses.

▼ *These students are enjoying their Easter vacation. They have chosen to attend a gymnasium to further their education.*

This girl, with friends nearby, is sitting on the bank of the River Neman. They belong to a Girl-Guide group and are glad to be on their Easter vacation. "We all attend the gymnasium," one of the girls says. Although they are allowed to leave school once they reach the age of 16, many children choose to continue their education at gymnasiums or vocational secondary schools, and around 7 percent go on to take undergraduate degrees at universities and colleges in Lithuania.

School holidays

The exact days of vacations in Lithuania can vary from school to school. However, the school year usually begins around September 1, and ends at the beginning of July. In between, students have one week off around the beginning of November, two weeks for Christmas, one week for Easter, as well as two months for summer vacation. There are also five days throughout the year that are public holidays, in which the schools are closed. These are all between November and May.

Higher education

The number of Lithuanian children going on to non-compulsory education is higher than that in the other Baltic states, Estonia and Latvia, and the country has a very high rate of literacy, at 99 percent.

The most important institution of higher education in Lithuania is Vilnius University, which is over 425 years old. Located in Kaunas are the Vitautas Magnus University, which is based on the American model of higher education, the University of Medicine, the University of Technology, the University of Agriculture, and the Veterinary Academy. Other universities can be found in Klaipeda and Siauliai.

▶ *The Kaunas gymnasium. Gymnasiums are secondary schools that specialize in subjects such as languages, sciences, and the arts.*

Cuisine

Lithuania does not have an extensive cuisine of its own, but there are a few traditional dishes. Food is related to the climate. Carrots, potatoes, and cabbages are the staple foods because they grow well in the Lithuanian climate.

These ingredients are turned into delicious meals. Although the dishes can be rather heavy and quite rich, this is suitable for the country, which has long cold winters during which hearty food is needed. Other agricultural products are sugar beets, corn, oats, and wheat, all of which are used in many recipes.

▲ *Potatoes are used in many recipes, including soups and zeppelins.*

Zeppelin

Cepelinai is a Lithuanian speciality. The word means "zeppelin," and the dish consists of a zeppelin-shaped parcel about eight inches long. It is made from mashed potatoes, mixed with a little flour to bind it together, with a filling of meat, bacon, and mushrooms. *Cepelinai* are cooked in water and are usually served with a sauce made from onions, butter, sour cream, and bacon pieces.

Another popular dish is potato cakes. They are made from shredded potatoes, mixed with flour and filled with a little meat. These small, thick cakes are served with sour cream.

Recipe for saltibarsciai (cold beet soup)

Ingredients
2 cooked beets, roughly grated
2 cucumbers
2 hard-boiled eggs
1 cup of sour cream
4 cups of buttermilk
1 cup of water
1 cup of finely chopped shallots or onions
1/2 dessertspoon of butter
1 pinch of salt
8 sprigs of fresh dill

Finely chop the hard-boiled egg yolks and mix with the shallots and a pinch of salt. Slice or grate the cucumber very finely and mix it with the sour cream, the buttermilk, the beets, and the water. Add this to the egg mixture and stir well. Garnish with finely chopped dill. Serve the cold soup with boiled potatoes and melted butter.

◄ *Saltibarsciai is a cold beet soup, one of Lithuania's traditional recipes.*

▶ *There is a lot of smoked fish in Lithuania, and many types of fish are preserved in this way.*

Fresh fish is only found served along the coastal region. Inland, fish is smoked or pickled in vinegar with onions, and sometimes cream. This way, the fish can be kept for a long time. In the past, when transportation was not as good as it is today, the fish would have spoiled on its journey inland to the restaurants and shops.

Popular dishes

Sauerkraut – a dish made from pickled white cabbage – is very popular in Lithuania and is served as an accompaniment to many meals. It is often combined with pork or bacon and potatoes. Peas with bacon or schnitzel are two favorite meals. Pork is the most common meat eaten in the country, although game meats such as hare, rabbit, and deer are also widely hunted and eaten in autumn and winter. A lot of this is sold to restaurants, where it is popular with both locals and tourists when cooked in traditional ways.

Lithuanians are fond of fresh produce, and they even gather foods such as mushrooms and berries themselves. This is something of a tradition, and whole families gather in the late summer and early autumn to take trips to the woodland areas, where these can be found in abundance. September is the best time to gather mushrooms, and there are many different types in Lithuania. At this time of year, there are hundreds of stands by the side of the roads selling freshly picked mushrooms.

Gathering summer fruits is also a popular pastime in the summer. These include wild strawberries, blackberries, and cowberries (only found in northern Europe, America and Asia). These berries are eaten fresh or made into jams which last all year round, for sandwiches or as a pancake filling. People sell these pots of homemade jams in the markets and on the streets.

◀ *In the autumn, people go to the forests and woodlands to gather wild mushrooms.*

Transportation

In general, the roads in Lithuania are well-maintained. Although many of them are quite narrow, they are kept in good condition and signs are clear. Large, four-lane highways have recently been constructed between Vilnius and Klaipeda, and Panevézys and Vilnius. The speed limit on these is 68 mph.

Railways

There are nearly 1,250 miles of railways in Lithuania. International trains run between the Baltic capitals; the service runs once a day. There are train connections to most cities, but the diesel and electric trains are not always very fast. First-, second-, and third-class tickets are available, and sometimes fourth-class. First-class coaches are only available on international trains.

▼ *Most sections of the railway have gone electric.*

The European highway E67 "Via Baltica" runs northward from Poland, and the route ends in Tallinn, Estonia. In Lithuania, it runs via Marijampole, Kaunas, and Panevézys to the Latvian border. Large parts of the road are being developed with financial assistance from the European Union. The government plans to extend the Via Baltica highway all the way to Helsinki, so a tunnel 50 miles long has to be built between Tallinn and Helsinki.

VIA BALTICA
KAUNO - MARIJAMPOLĖS -
SUVALKŲ KELIO ir
MARIJAMPOLĖS SANKRYŽŲ
REKONSTRUKCIJA

Projektą finansavo
EUROPOS SĄJUNGA ir

LIETUVOS RESPUBLIKA

Užsakovas:
Lietuvos
automobilių
kelių direkcija

Rangovas:
UAB "ALKESTA"

2003m.

Buses

Buses are also available in the cities, but they are infrequent and can be slow. On shorter routes, small minibuses are used, which can hold around 15 passengers. These stop on request.

In Vilnius and Kaunas, trolleybuses are available and are the best way to travel. Trams are not common in Lithuania, and there are no subways.

Ferries

Another way of traveling to other European countries from places in Lithuania is by ferry. These leave from the port of Klaipeda, and go to Stockholm in Sweden, and to Kiel, Travemünde, and Mukran in Germany.

◀ Passenger ferries travel from the ports in Lithuania's coastal regions to other European destinations.

Aviation

Lithuania has two airlines. The largest is Lithuanian Airlines. This offers daily flights to Amsterdam, Copenhagen, Stockholm, Helsinki, London, Brussels, Berlin, Frankfurt, Tallinn, Moscow, and Kiev. The airport is located about three miles from Vilnius. The other airline company is Air Lithuania. From the airport near Kaunas, flights are available to Palanga, on the coast, and from there to foreign destinations: Malmö in Sweden, Billund in Denmark, Hamburg in Germany, and Oslo in Norway.

▲ Passengers board a Lithuanian Airlines plane.

◄ Vilnius Airport opened in 1944. In 2004, nearly one million people used the airport.

▼ Palanga Airport is in western Lithuania, near the Baltic coast.

The economy

In the past, agriculture and forestry were major parts of the Lithuanian economy. Today, about 20 percent of the working population are active in agriculture – far less than it used to be. Industry accounts for 30 percent of the labor force, and services 50 percent.

▼ *Harvesting begins at the end of August. Most of the work is done by machinery.*

Agriculture and forestry

Nearly half of Lithuania's land is used for plowing. The most important agricultural products are potatoes, sugar beets, cabbages, and carrots. In addition, corn, oats, and wheat are grown.

About 16 percent of the country's land is used for forestry. Coniferous trees are especially important for the timber trade. There are farms with dairy cows and beef cattle, pig farms, and poultry farms.

◄ *Potatoes are dug up by hand almost everywhere. This requires a large manual workforce.*

▼ *Wood and wood products make up 5 percent of Lithuania's export products.*

Industry

Important industrial sectors are the chemical industry (producing fertilizers), metal-cutting machine tools, electronics, and construction materials. Factories produce shoe polish, car wax, carpet cleaner, and glue. One large factory, with more than 4,000 employees, manufactures cathode-ray tubes for televisions. Light industry around the cities produces textiles (linen and wool), wood, paper, and leather goods. The food industry produces canned food and sugar. Many factories also produce fabric, clothing, curtains, shoes, and sweets.

▲ *A modern textile factory. Textiles are an important light industry in Lithuania.*

Currency

While the Lithuanian government has agreed in the future to adopt western Europe's currency, the euro, for now the currency of the country is the lita. Each lita is divided into 100 centas. Litas are available in banknotes of 2, 5, 10, 20, 50, 100 and 200. Coins are available in 1, 2 and 5 lita pieces. There are around three litas to one U.S. dollar.

◀ *The 20-lita note has a picture of Jonas Maciulis, a famous Lithuanian poet and pioneer of the renaissance in Lithuanian language and culture in literature.*

◀ *Oil is an important import and export commodity. There is an oil refinery in Mazakiai that processes unrefined oil into oil products like gasoline and diesel fuel. Much of this goes to Kaliningrad.*

Import and export

Russia used to be Lithuania's most important trading partner. The collapse of the Russian economy in the late 1990s naturally had an effect on Lithuania's economy. However, it made a speedy recovery and, Lithuania has increasingly focused on other European countries. Lithuania's most important import and export partners are Germany, Poland, Denmark, and the other Baltic countries, Estonia and Latvia.

▼ *Hydroelectric power plants like this one generate nearly 4 percent of the country's power.*

◄ While churches and other old buildings characterize the old city in Vilnius, the outer regions are dominated by skyscrapers, shopping centers, and industrial areas.

The main imports are mineral products (around 21 percent). As in the past, oil and gas still have to be imported from Russia. Machines, cars, and equipment make up around 17 percent of all imports. Although there are still many old cars, buses, and trucks on the roads, increasing numbers of the latest models can be seen. Another sign of Lithuania's much-improved economy is the large buildings that are rapidly appearing everywhere. Many houses and buildings are being renovated.

Mineral products make up 25 percent of all exports. Textiles and clothing are the second-largest group, at around 16 percent. Other exports from the country include machinery and equipment, chemical products such as varnish and glue, wood, and food products.

Transporting goods

When Russia lost the Baltic states, it also lost many of its major ports. The seaport of Klaipeda has consequently become an important place for transportation of Russian products. The roads leading to the port are in excellent condition, and there is also a good rail connection to Klaipeda. Lithuania's location on the Baltic coast allows much trade to take place via sea as well as land.

▶ *A pilot boat in the port of Klaipeda*

Tourism

Winter comes early in Lithuania, and the tourist season is short, from May to September. In this regard, the climate is not ideal for vacationers looking for year-round sunshine. However, in the summer months, it is a pleasant place to visit.

▼ *New shops continue to open in the cities, as more and more visitors come to Lithuania each tourist season.*

Lithuania is not yet a popular tourist destination, but since the country's independence, growing numbers of people have traveled to this part of Europe. Tourism is an increasingly important part of the Lithuanian economy. This has been aided by the country's membership in the European Union since 2004.

Tourists come to Lithuania to enjoy nature and the historical sites. Because the country is not very densely populated, it can be peaceful compared with other tourist destinations.

▼ *The capital, Vilnius, on the River Neris, attracts most tourists because of its old buildings and churches.*

Popular destinations

Although there is a lot of open countryside in Lithuania, the towns and cities still attract the most foreign visitors. Vilnius is the most popular destination – an attractive city on the confluence of two rivers. Kaunas and Klaipeda, with its sandy beaches, are also popular with tourists. Inland, the national parks draw visitors who go to enjoy the peace and quiet.

▲ *The rustic villages are calm and peaceful, offering an escape from the bustle of the cities.*

▼ *The Town Hall Square in Kaunas has many historical buildings.*

▶ *An entrance ticket to the famous Trakai History Museum (see page 21), which is located in the beautiful Trakai Castle, built in 1409*

There are several spas and health resorts in Lithuania. These attract visitors from other parts of the country, as well as foreigners, who go to enjoy the mineral baths in peaceful settings.

Druskininkai is the largest and best-known resort. The town is located in the south of Lithuania, just four miles from the Belarus border. Built on the River Neman, the town is surrounded by woods. The air is clean and healthy, and the resort offers saline mineral baths. People have been visiting the waters here since the seventeenth century, but the town gained its international reputation in 1794, when the Polish king declared the area a health resort. Construction began on baths and bath houses almost immediately, and the resort grew extremely popular under the rule of Tsar Nicholas I.

Today, the resort is still fully operational and is visited especially by people with heart conditions or respiratory problems, who benefit from the extremely salty water.

▲ One of the buildings in the Druskininkai resort, a town set in a tranquil woodland environment

▼ Birštonas is a resort town in southern Lithuania and is renowned for its beauty. It offers treatments using peat and mineral waters.

▶ Bath houses and health resorts are located in peaceful, park-like surroundings.

Who visits Lithuania?

In 2004, about ten percent of the visitors to Lithuania were from western European countries. Most of the people visited the larger cities or the coast. The table below gives information about the most popular places to visit in Lithuania, and percentages of tourists in each place.

Most of the tourists stayed in the capital and in the city of Kaunas. The coastal resorts were also popular – the seaside resort Palanga, the port of Klaipeda, and the area near Neringa. The health resort, Druskininkai, was another favorite place to stay.

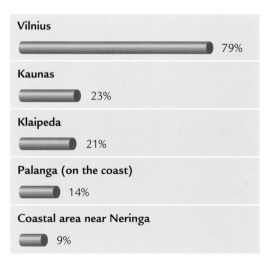

Vilnius
79%

Kaunas
23%

Klaipeda
21%

Palanga (on the coast)
14%

Coastal area near Neringa
9%

◀ Old wooden houses can be seen all across Lithuania. Many of them are no longer in use, but they are still standing in the countryside as a reminder of times past.

How do they get there?

In 1996, 832,000 tourists visited Lithuania –
40 percent went by road (by car or bus),
39 percent went by train, 13 percent by airplane,
and 8 percent by boat.

In 2002, the number of tourists was considerably
higher – 1,428,000 people visited Lithuania,
a rise of more than 70 percent in six years.

▼ *The hotels and bed and breakfast lodgings are not
only found in the big cities. There are also some in the
middle of the woods, edging the dunes, and close to
the beaches of Palanga.*

Latvia	29%
Russia	24%
Belarus	14%
Poland	10%
Estonia	7%
Germany	4%
Other Russian states	2%
Slovakia, Hungary	2%
Finland	1.5%
Rest of the world	6.5%

▲ *Tourists stroll
along a pier, enjoy-
ing the sunshine.*

◄ *The countries
of origin of tourists
in 2004*

Holiday	34%
Visit to friends or relatives	31%
Business	23%
Other	12%

◄ *The purpose
of people's visits
to Lithuania
in 2004*

Nature

Shortly after the Ice Age, when the first people moved into Lithuanian territory, the area was a boggy landscape in which only a few grasses and shrubs could survive. Over the centuries, the land grew drier and the first trees – birches – took root.

▼ *In winter, the boggy areas are iced over. They do not start to thaw out until April.*

Later on, oaks and, in the coastal areas, pine trees and spruces, began to flourish. Although large parts of Lithuania were eventually covered with trees, the area remained abundant in water. The country is still characterized by rivers and lakes. Several areas are made up of wetlands that are now protected because of the wildlife they support.

◄ *The first flowers emerge in the forests and woodlands in April, after the long winter.*

The forests and wetlands are much-prized in Lithuania today. However, as human settlements were established, people began to need more farmland, and they started cutting down areas of woodland. Today, only about 25 percent of Lithuanian territory is still forested. Deforestation is a key environmental issue being addressed in the twenty-first century.

The woods that remain are varied, with different species of trees, including maple, birch, beech, lime, and aspen. Only a few of the old oak trees are left. Among the trees grow shrubs with edible berries, such as bilberries and blackberries. There are also several different species of wild mushrooms that grow on the forest floors.

▲ *Wild mushrooms grow in the forests and woods. Not all mushrooms are safe to eat, but Lithuanian people gather the edible ones in the autumn.*

► *The woods are interspersed with fast-flowing streams, and are an ideal habitat for birds.*

◀ *Wolves are shy animals by nature, but in the winter they can be seen on the outskirts of villages, searching for food.*

▼ *Water birds like gulls live along the coastal regions.*

Animals

The woods are the habitat of many large animals – red deer, roe deer, elk and, wild boar – besides predators, such as the fox, wolf, bear, and lynx. Smaller animals such as rabbits, hares, ermines, martens, and polecats also live in the woods and fields.

Around 300 different bird species are found in Lithuania. These include birds of prey, songbirds, snipes, and many kinds of water birds. In the woods, woodpeckers and various songbirds can be found, such as finches and thrushes. Birds of prey common in Lithuania include owls, goshawks, buzzards, and eagles.

Lapwings, swans, and herons can also be observed frequently. The southern lake district is an important breeding area. Gulls, cormorants, and other water birds live along the coast. Seals and porpoises swim in the coastal waters.

▶ *The brown bear is one of the predators found in parts of Lithuania.*

◄ *Storks are summer guests in Lithuania. They arrive in April and make the long migratory trip to Africa in September.*

Besides a lot of fish – especially carp, bream, perch, and trout – otters can be found in the rivers. Perch is the favorite fish dish of the Lithuanians.

Environmental issues

One of the main environmental issues at the moment is the nuclear plant in Ignalina, which was designed and built during the Soviet period. After the Chernobyl disaster, in which nuclear radiation leaked from a plant in the Ukraine, people demanded that the Ignalina plant be shut down. Measures are being taken to achieve this, although it is unlikely to happen until 2009. Large sums of money from the European Union have been spent on safety measures. The plant generates 80 percent of Lithuania's energy resources, so a solution to the energy problem needs to be found.

▼ *The nuclear power plant in Ignalina*

In 1989, the French National Geographic Institute declared that the middle of Europe lay approximately nine miles to the north of Vilnius. A sculpture park was laid out in the heart of the woods, known as the Europos Parkas. The exact center of Europe is pinpointed with a pyramid-shaped sculpture. However, several other countries, including Slovakia, also lay claim to having the center of Europe. This calculation did not include European Russia, however.

▲ *This pyramid claims to mark the geographical center of Europe, although other countries also lay claim to this.*

National Parks

Lithuania has five national parks, and several protected nature reserves. The parks have been established in order to protect large areas of the natural environment from human interference, including deforestation and destruction of natural habitats. In the parks, it is illegal to cut down trees, light fires, catch or hunt animals, destroy plants and shrubs, or pick rare species of flowers and plants.

The landscape in park areas is varied, with hills, valleys, lakes, and woods. Most of them have walking and cycle paths, and this is often the best way to enjoy Lithuania's natural environment. It is possible to drive through some of the national parks and nature reserves, and there are also waterways on which visitors can travel through the area by canoe.

The Aukštaitija National Park covers a historical area of Lithuania close to the borders with Latvia and Belarus, about 68 miles north of Vilnius. The park was established in 1974 in an effort to prevent the construction of the nuclear power plant in the nearby town of Ignalina. The plant was built anyway, but Aukštaitija remains an important reservation.

▶ *The entrance to the Aukštaitija National Park*

The park covers an area of more than 100,000 acres. About half of all Lithuanian plant species can be found here, including 70 types of water plants, many of them very rare. Almost all the animal species found in Lithuania roam the Aukštaitija National Park – fox, wolf, elk, wild boar, and many more. White mountain hares also live here, but they can be difficult to spot in the winter months when snow covers the ground.

Dzukijos Park is the largest national park, located in the south and bordering Belarus. It is an isolated spot – towns and villages are sparse – and it is abundant with water in the form of hundreds of lakes and ponds. Right in the middle of the park lies the oldest wooded marshland in Lithuania. More than 150 different species of birds live here.

Trakai National Park is located near Vilnius. Centuries ago, Trakai was the capital of Lithuania, until in 1323, Grand Duke Gediminas transferred the capital to Vilnius. The old city has a rich history and is located in a beautiful scenic area, on a long and narrow peninsula where three lakes meet: Lake Galvè, Lake Totoriskis and Lake Lukos. There are still many old, wooden houses. The castle is located at the near end of the peninsula and it can be reached by way of wooden bridge.

Žemaitija National Park is the most recently established. The area consists of woodlands (nearly 50 percent), wetlands, and a large lake.

▼ *The castle at Trakai stands on a peninsula where three lakes meet.*

▲ *It is only a five-minute journey by ferry from Klaipeda to the Kuršiu Nerija National Park.*

Kuršiu Nerija National Park is located near the port of Klaipeda. It consists of a sandy stretch of land along the coast, 61 miles long and from 1,312 feet to 2 miles wide. The area was created about 5,000 years ago, by a combination of the wind, ocean currents and the estuarial current of the River Neman. An inlet, the Curonian Lagoon, has formed, with a narrow sea gate near Klaipeda. The water of the inlet is fresh rather than saltwater. A few settlements are located on the sandy spit. In the past, amber was found here, and fishermen used to live in the settlements. A large number of dunes are covered with woodland, but the highest dune (197 feet) is bare.

▶ *The highest dune in the Kuršiu Nerija National Park is 197 feet high.*

Glossary

Communism A political system based on the principles of government ownership of property.

Concentration camp Prison camps where Jews and other minority groups were sent by the Germans during the Second World War.

Constitution A series of laws outlining the basic principles of a government or country.

Hanseatic League A group of German-owned towns that formed an economic and defensive unit under the control of wealthy merchants.

Orthodox Church The Christian Church in the East; it has several independent branches, including Russian and Greek Orthodox.

Prussia A former kingdom in north-central Europe, including north Germany and northern Poland.

Serfdom A social system in which laborers (serfs) were bound to a particular area of land owned by a landlord. Serfs were not slaves because they could not be sold.

Stone Age The earliest period in technological history, when tools and weapons were made from stone.

Index

Websites

http://www.lonelyplanet.com/destinations/europe/lithuania/
http://www.cia.gov/cia/publications/factbook/geos/lh.html
http://www.ltembassyus.org/
http://www.dfat.gov.au/geo/lithuania/

Eu

Iceland

N
W E
S

A T L A N T I C   O C E A N

NORTH SE

Republic
of
Ireland

United Kingdom

The N

Belgium

Luxe

France

Switze

Portugal

Monac

Spain

MEDITERRANE

0   500 km

0   500 miles